The Adventures of Grammy and Sammy

By
Suzetta Perkins & Samayya Walters

Illustrated by
Jacquelyn Scott

The Adventures of Grammy and Sammy
Copyright © 2015 by Suzetta Perkins & Samayya Walters
ISBN: 978-0-9965986-3-7
LCCN: 2015960927
First Edition
Printed in the United States of America

2 4 6 8 10 9 7 5 3 1

Interior design & layout by Cranberry Quill Publishing
Illustrated by: Jacquelyn Scott
Photo credits: Eric Stevenson at www.evaporsshow.com

Published by:
Cranberry Quill Publishing
A Division of GibbsBiz, Incorporated
111 Lamon Street, Suite 204, Fayetteville, NC 28301
www.CranberryQuill.com

Author Samayya Walters
Bio

Samayya Walters was born in Honolulu, Hawaii. She is the eldest daughter of Teliza and Willie Walters. She has a younger sister, Maliah. Samayya is a 7th grader at Richmond Hill Middle School in Richmond Hill, Georgia, just south of Savannah.

Samayya is the co-author of *The Adventures of Grammy and Sammy,* along with her grandmother, Suzetta Perkins, who's the author of ten fictional novels. Four years ago, Samayya and her grandmother, sometimes affectionately known as GG, which stands for gorgeous grandma, sat down and began to write stories about their adventures. Samayya is an award-winning writer in her own rite, having received the Excellence in Writing Award two years In a row, when she was a student at Holly Hill Elementary School in Enterprise, Alabama.

While it's not surprising, Samayya has many other talents. She designs and sews, with many of her creations coming from the top of her head and also with the help of YouTube. Her fashions are what some would call *Project Runway* ready. Samayya also loves to create videos; one such video was made to a Michael Jackson sound track.

One of Samayya's proudest accomplishments was that she made the Cheerleading squad at Richmond Hill Middle School her first year there. Look out for more from this author.

Author Suzetta Perkins
Bio

A native of Oakland, California, Suzetta Perkins resides in Fayetteville, North Carolina. She is the mother of two grown children, Teliza and Gerald, and two granddaughters, Samayya and Maliah. Samayya is the co-author of *The Adventures of Grammy and Sammy.*

Writing has always been in her blood. While a senior in high school, Suzetta realized her first published work in her high school yearbook, in which she was co-editor.

Suzetta penned her first novel, *Behind the Veil,* in 2000, and it was published in 2006. Since then, she has published nine more novels that include *A Love So Deep, Ex-Terminator: Life After Marriage, Déjà vu, Nothing Stays the Same, Betrayed, At the End of the Day, In My Rearview Mirror, Silver Bullets,* and *Hollywood Skye,* which will be released in December 2015. Suzetta is also a contributing author of *My Soul to His Spirit,* an anthology that received the 2006 Fresh Voices Award and was featured in the 2005 issue of *Ebony* magazine. Besides writing, Suzetta's other passions are reading and scrapbooking.

Four years ago, she and granddaughter, Samayya, sat down and began to write stories about their adventures. Samayya, an award-winning writer in her own rite, penned and had editing rights in one-hundred percent of *The Adventures of Grammy and Sammy.*

Suzetta is the President and co-founder of the Sistahs Book Club. She's also the Secretary of the University at Fayetteville State University in Fayetteville, North Carolina, her alma mater.

INTRODUCTION

Samantha Washington, better known as, Sammy to her family, has a wonderful relationship with her grandmother. Her family consists of her father, Captain Russell Washington; her mother, Bridget Washington; and her brother, Russell Jr., whose nickname is Rusty. Captain Washington is in the military and stationed at Fort Rucker, Alabama, but he'll soon receive military orders to report to Fort Bragg, North Carolina.

Suzie Porter, aka Grammy, as her grandchildren call her, is Bridget Washington's mother, and she lives in Fayetteville, North Carolina. Sammy loves to spend time with Grammy because she loves to do fun things. It won't be long before Sammy's family moves to North Carolina and she'll be able to see Grammy more often.

The Adventures of Grammy and Sammy chronicles some of the fun things they do together, but there are also lessons to be learned as we follow them on their different adventures. Grammy and Sammy's adventures show the love between two people—one very young and the other much, much older. Wisdom is what Grammy passes down to Sammy in many teachable moments. Pure love and an inquisitive, quirky sense of a young girl growing up in today's society is what Grammy receives in return.

THE ADVENTURES OF GRAMMY AND SAMMY

TABLE OF CONTENTS

Grammy and Sammy's Thanksgiving

It was three days before Thanksgiving. Sammy's family was going to Grammy's house for Thanksgiving dinner.

Sammy loves going to Grammy's house; she has so much fun. Grammy is going to cook Thanksgiving dinner. She is going to fix turkey and dressing, glazed ham and candied yams, collard greens, and macaroni and cheese. Best of all, she will bake sweet potato pies and Sammy's favorite, ambrosia. Grammy and Sammy will have the best time.

Sammy has an idea and wants to tell Grammy right away. When Sammy's mom, Bridget, called Grammy, Sammy asked if she could speak with her.

"Hi, Grammy," Sammy said.

"Hello, Sammy. How are you?" Grammy asked.

"I'm fine. I can't wait to see you."

"I can't wait to see you either, Sammy. I love you."

"I love you, too. Grammy, may I ask you a question?"

"Of course, baby. You can always ask Grammy a question. What do you have on your mind?"

"Grammy," Sammy began as if she was afraid to ask the question. "When I come to North Carolina, will you please take me to your beauty shop to get my hair washed and curled?"

Grammy began to laugh. "Yes, baby. I will make an appointment for us."

"Thank you, Grammy." Sammy was so happy.

"You're welcome."

Sammy hung up the telephone and jumped up and down with joy. Sammy couldn't wait to go to Grammy's for Thanksgiving.

"Mommy, can we go to Grammy's house now?" Sammy asked.

"No, you'll have to wait until it's time to go. We plan to leave on Wednesday."

"But today is Monday." Bridget patted Sammy on the head.

Sammy didn't want to wait any longer. Every time she asked her mother if they could go to Grammy's early, she got the same answer—no.

On Tuesday morning, Sammy was up early. She went into the living room and picked up her mother's cell phone and called Grammy.

"Hi, Grammy," Sammy said. "I'm ready to come to your house now."

"That's fantastic, Sammy. Where's Mommy?" There was a pause. "Oh, she didn't give you permission to use the telephone."

Panic was in Sammy's voice. "No," Sammy said, her voice trembling. She hung up the telephone abruptly.

A few seconds later, Sammy's parents woke up and announced that they were leaving for North Carolina today. Oh, wasn't Sammy surprised. Now she wished she hadn't called Grammy. Maybe Grammy wouldn't tell her parents.

Sammy's parents put their suitcases in the car and began the trip to North Carolina from Alabama. Sammy worried the whole trip about Grammy telling her mother and father about using the cell phone without their permission. When her parents stopped at Burger King for lunch, Sammy couldn't eat.

"What's wrong, Sammy?" her mother asked. "I thought you would be happy that we were going to Grammy's house early. And why aren't you eating?"

Sammy shrugged her shoulders.

"You need to eat something," Bridget said to Sammy. "Look at Rusty. He's gobbled down all of his hamburger and fries. We'll be at Grammy's soon."

Sammy ate the hamburger. Before long, she fell asleep. It seemed as if Sammy had been asleep a long time when the car suddenly jerked to a stop. Her eyes opened and her father hollered out.

"We're here! We're at Grammy's house."

Everyone was happy to see Grammy. Sammy should have been the happiest of all. When Sammy saw her, Grammy winked.

Grammy hugged Sammy and gave her a kiss. Then she whispered in her ear. "Your secret is safe with me...this time. Remember, you must always ask your parents if you can use the telephone."

Sammy smiled and hugged Grammy. "Thank you, Grammy."

"You're welcome."

Everyone went into the house. It was so warm and cozy. They found their rooms, freshened up, and ate dinner. Instead of watching TV, everyone talked and then went to bed. There was a lot to do to help Grammy get Thanksgiving dinner ready.

The next morning, Sammy was up bright and early to help Grammy. So was her mother, Bridget.

Sammy turned to her mother and smiled. "Thank you, Mommy, for asking Dad to come to Grammy's house early. Now Grammy doesn't have to do all of the work. We can help her."

Sammy's mother smiled. "You're welcome, Sammy. I would never let Grammy do all of the work. I've baked pies and cakes that your dad took out of the car."

"Uhmm," Sammy said. "Mommy makes good pies and cakes." Then Sammy looked up at Grammy. Grammy only smiled.

"I have a confession to make, Mommy."

Bridget looked confused. "Oh. What are you confessing?"

"I...I called Grammy this morning to tell her I wanted to come today. I'm sorry for using your cell phone without asking."

Bridget glanced at Grammy and then back at Sammy. "I'm glad you told me the truth. You should never use my cell phone without asking. It costs money to make a phone call."

"Oh," Sammy said in surprise. "I didn't know."

"Now you do, but that goes for anything that doesn't belong to you. I hope you've learned your lesson."

In a very low voice, Sammy said, "Yes, I've learned my lesson."

"We're going to leave that behind us and help Grammy with Thanksgiving dinner."

"Thanks, Mommy."

The next day, everyone dressed up for the Thanksgiving feast. Sammy's family came to the table with their mouths wide open. Grammy cooked everything Sammy liked, even her favorite dessert.

When everyone was seated at the table, Sammy's father, Russell Sr., said grace. He thanked the heavenly Father for the food that Grammy and Bridget cooked for Thanksgiving Day. He was also thankful for arriving safely at Grammy's. It was the best Thanksgiving ever.

LESSON

Ask before using something that doesn't belong to you. It may cost money to use it.

There's a consequence to your actions, whether good or bad.

WHAT LESSON DID YOU LEARN?

Grammy and Sammy's Trip to the Beauty Shop

Beauty is in the eye of the beholder. Grammy smiled when she looked at her granddaughter, Sammy. No one could tell Grammy that she didn't have the most beautiful granddaughter in the world; she already knew it.

At Thanksgiving dinner, Grammy couldn't shake the thought of how much Sammy looked like her mother, Bridget, when she was Sammy's age. Bridget was Grammy's daughter. Her head full of black, wavy hair and that radiant smile always warmed Grammy's heart.

Today, Sammy and Grammy were going to the beauty shop to get their hair shampooed and curled. Sammy called Grammy before her family came to visit and asked Grammy if she would take her to the beauty shop to make her hair pretty. Grammy smiled. This was another wonderful way to spend time with her granddaughter, even if it was going to cost her a few dollars.

Grammy and Sammy set out for the beauty shop. Sammy began to sing one of her favorite songs by Selena Gomez. "Who says, who says you're not pretty, who says you're not beautiful, who says you're not perfect..."

"Always remember the words to that song," Grammy began. "You are perfect, you are pretty, and you are beautiful in God's eyes, your mommy's eyes, and Grammy's eyes. Don't let anyone tell you any different."

Sammy had a big smile on her face. "Mommy told me the same thing."

When Grammy and Sammy arrived at the beauty shop, Ms. Riley, the beautician, gave Grammy a hug and patted Sammy on her head.

"Your granddaughter is so beautiful," Ms. Riley said to Grammy.

"I told Sammy that very thing only minutes before we came in here. She's beautiful like her mother."

"Thank you," Sammy said and smiled.

"Okay, Sammy," Ms. Riley said. "I'm going to shampoo your hair first."

Sammy followed Ms. Riley to the shampoo bowl and laid her head back after Ms. Riley put the shampoo bib around her. Ms. Riley took special care with her hair, as it was very soft.

Ms. Riley lathered Sammy's hair and gave it a good scrub. She rinsed, conditioned, and rinsed it again. Once all of the shampoo and conditioner were out, Ms. Riley took a towel and blotted Sammy's hair dry. Sammy smiled and Grammy smiled back.

Next, Ms. Riley moved Sammy to another chair and began to blow dry her hair. Sammy had a head full of hair that fell below her shoulders. When Ms. Riley finished, Sammy's hair was straight and silky. Sammy reached up and felt her hair. She turned to look at Grammy who gave her a wink.

Sammy wanted curls all over her head. The curls made Sammy look like a princess. When Ms. Riley finished curling Sammy's hair, she gave Sammy a mirror.

Ms. Riley turned the chair Sammy was sitting in so she could see how pretty the back of her hair looked. With the mirror facing Sammy, she held it up to see what it looked like in the mirror on the wall. Sammy was pleased.

"You're all finished, Sammy, and it's time to make Grammy look good," Ms. Riley said.

Sammy was still admiring herself in the mirror. "Thank you for making me beautiful."

"You were already beautiful," Ms. Riley reminded her. "I only gave you a power boost."

Sammy covered her face with her hands and laughed. Then she watched Ms. Riley work magic with Grammy by repeating the process all over again. When Ms. Riley finished with Grammy's hair, she looked beautiful too.

"How much will that be?" Grammy asked.

"Your cost today is seventy dollars."

Sammy bucked her eyes and looked at Grammy. "That's a lot of money."

"Everything costs," Grammy said. "The gas we used to drive to the beauty shop cost money. All the products Ms. Riley used on our hair cost money. It costs to make us look good, but we are worth it."

Sammy smiled. "Thank you, Grammy, for spending your hard earned money to make us look beautiful."

"You're welcome. We will have to do this again. Now tell Ms. Riley goodbye."

"Bye, Ms. Riley. Thank you."

"You're welcome, Sammy. Now you need somewhere to go."

"Yes, Grammy. Can we go and get something to eat?"

"We have Thanksgiving leftovers at home. It costs to eat out."

"I forgot," Sammy said, putting her hand over her mouth. "I'm sorry, Grammy. You just spent money to make my hair pretty."

"Let me think about it a second. I guess we can go somewhere for a treat, especially since we both look pretty in our new hairdos."

"It's my fault," Ms. Riley said. "I opened my big mouth."

"No," Grammy said. "I wanted Sammy to learn a lesson...that everything costs. I believe she understands, and now we're on our way to Red Robin to have hamburgers, fries, and something to drink."

"Yeah," Sammy said, jumping in the air. "Grammy, you're the best."

LESSON

Beauty lies within each of us.
Everything costs something.

WHAT LESSON DID YOU LEARN?

Grammy and Sammy Go to the Restaurant

No one would have guessed that Grammy was Sammy's grandmother. Grammy had a young looking face and she wore the latest fashions and hairdos. Sammy's hair was full of pretty, bouncy curls that were the handiwork of Ms. Riley, the beautician. Since Grammy and Sammy wanted to show off their new hairdos, Grammy drove to one of Sammy's favorite restaurants, Red Robin.

"Today was a good day, Grammy. I had the best time."

"Well, in order to keep your hair looking nice, you have to treat it nice. That means you have to brush it every day and put it in hair rollers before you go to bed each night. By doing so, your hair will remain pretty for a few days. If you don't..." Grammy began.

"It will look terrible," Sammy blurted out, "and you will have wasted all of your money."

Grammy smiled.

"Am I right, Grammy?"

"Yes, you learned the lesson well, Sammy. I'm pleased. Now it's time to get something to eat."

Grammy and Sammy arrived at the restaurant and were shown to a booth. Sammy shook her head *no* when the waitress tried to give her a balloon. Sammy was much too old for balloons.

"I already know what I want, Grammy."

"You do?"

"Yes. I'm allergic to so many things, and I don't have many choices."

"I'm glad that you're being careful about what you eat."

The waitress came to the table and took their orders. "I'll have water with lemon," Grammy said. "And my granddaughter will have a Sprite."

"Your granddaughter?" the waitress asked. "You look like mother and daughter." The waitress squinted her eyes to give Grammy another once over.

"My Grammy takes good care of herself," Sammy interjected.

The waitress smiled and nodded her head. "Do you ladies know what you'd like to order?"

"Yes, Sammy said. "I'll have a hamburger...no mayonnaise. And I want French fries."

"Are you going to eat your burger plain?" the waitress asked, as she stared at Sammy.

"I have food allergies and I have to be careful what I eat."

"It's great that you are aware of what you can and cannot eat. And what would you like?" the waitress asked Grammy.

"I'll have an avocado, bacon, cheeseburger with French fries."

"Great," the waitress said. "I'll put your orders in, and they should be up very soon. In the meantime, I'll get your drinks."

"I have so much fun when I visit you, Grammy. I get to experience different things."

"I'm sure you and your mother have had other experiences that have also been fun."

"I do. It's just that you like to go more than Mommy. I'll be glad when we move to North Carolina."

"Grammy looked at Sammy and smiled. "I'll be glad when your family moves here as well. That means I'll get to see you more often."

"And we can do more fun things."

"It certainly does. Maybe we can include your mother in on one of our adventures."

"She would like that."

"Look, Sammy. Our food is coming."

"That was quick; I'm hungry."

The waitress sat Sammy's hamburger and fries in front of her and then sat Grammy's food down, followed by their drinks.

"This looks good," Sammy said, rubbing her stomach.

"It does," Grammy replied. "But what should we do before we take the first bite?"

"We say a blessing and thank God for providing us with good food."

Grammy smiled. "Good, girl."

"May I say grace?" Sammy asked.

"Yes. I would love for you to say grace," Grammy said.

Sammy closed her eyes and brought her hands together. "Thank You, Lord, for the food that we just ordered. Let it be good and nourishing to our bodies. May Grammy have enough money to pay for it. Amen."

Grammy opened her eyes and began to laugh. "That was a good prayer, Sammy. And it was honest."

"Thank you, Grammy. I love you."

"I love you too. Now let's eat."

LESSON

In order to have something nice, you have to take care of it. In order for Sammy to keep her new hairdo nice, she has to brush it and roll it in curlers every night.

WHAT LESSON DID YOU LEARN?

Sammy Moves to North Carolina

Sammy was very happy. Today, her family was moving to North Carolina from Alabama. The movers had already picked up her family's furniture and now she would get to see her Grammy Sue all the time.

Sammy's father, Russell Sr., was in the military, and he was being stationed at Fort Bragg, North Carolina. Fort Bragg is very close to Grammy's house. Sammy's mother, Bridget, was excited, too. She would be able to see her mother more often. She was more than ready to leave Alabama.

Sammy and her brother, Rusty, (short for Russell, Jr.), entertained themselves while Russell, Sr. navigated through traffic on Interstate 20.

"Let's play the letter game," Sammy said to Rusty. "Let's start with the letter A. My word is airplane."

"Augusta," Rusty said, as they passed the highway sign that announced they were in the city of Augusta.

"That wasn't fair," Sammy said. "You cheated."

"No, I didn't. Now what's your word?"

"Apple."

"Automobile."

"Animal."

"Ape."

"I'm tired of playing this game," Sammy said, letting out a sigh. "Let's count the number of license plates from the different states."

"Georgia," Rusty shouted.

"South Carolina," Sammy countered, pointing at a car that whizzed by.

"North Carolina."

"New York."

They went on like this for the next ten miles.

"It's time for the two of you to take a break," Bridget said. "We will be at Grammy's house in about three and a half hours and that will depend upon how fast your dad drives. I'm going to put in a movie."

"I want to see *Monsters, Inc.*," Sammy said.

"No, let's see *Spiderman*."

"Why don't you compromise?" Bridget said, raising her hand as if it was a white flag of surrender. "You can watch *Monsters, Inc.* first and then watch *Spiderman*."

"Okay," Rusty said with his mouth stuck out.

Sammy and Rusty sat back and watched the movie and were silent for the next couple of hours.

"I have to go the bathroom," Sammy said out loud, as soon as the movie was over. "I have to go real bad."

"We are a few miles from Florence, South Carolina, and we'll stop there. We'll eat and take our bathroom break. After that, we're getting back in the car and won't stop again until we get to Grammy's house."

"Yeah," Sammy said. "I can't wait to see Grammy again."

Getting into the car after their bathroom break, Sammy and Rusty sat back and watched *Spiderman*. Even before the movie was over, they both fell asleep. When they woke up, Russell, Sr. was pulling into Grammy's driveway. Grammy waved her hands. Everyone was excited to see Grammy.

The Washingtons would be moving into housing at Fort Bragg Army Military Base as soon as Russell, Sr. checked in and met with housing. The best thing of all was that they would be near Grammy.

LESSON

Compromise is good.

WHAT LESSON DID YOU LEARN?

Grammy and Sammy Have Fun Shopping

Grammy and Sammy love being together. They say funny things and make each other laugh.

"Let's go shopping," Grammy said.

"Yeah," Sammy said with enthusiasm. "That's one of my favorite things to do."

Grammy drove to Walmart and she and Sammy looked around. They saw pretty, spring dresses that would be perfect for Sammy. Sammy selected one and put it in the cart. Grammy also picked up some bananas, red apples, and a bag of potato chips along the way.

"Grammy, may we go to the book section? I love to read."

"I love to read, too," Grammy said. "Maybe I'll find something I like to read as well."

Sammy and Grammy pushed the shopping cart to the book section. There were so many books to choose from. Sammy picked up several books until she found the one she wanted to buy. "May I have this book, Grammy?"

Grammy took the book from Sammy, read the title, and thumbed through it. "It looks like a book that is suitable for you to read."

"I have ten Junie B. Jones books. Did you find something you like to read?"

"Yes, I did." Grammy found a cookbook to add to her collection. "I have so many books at home already that I haven't read yet, but I can't resist this cookbook. We have a book for you and a cookbook for me. Now it's time for us to go to the register and pay for our items."

Sammy was happy. She pushed the cart for Grammy and found a lane where they wouldn't have to wait long to check out. When it was their turn, Sammy helped Grammy place the dress, fruit, potato chips, and books on the conveyor. Sammy watched as the grocery clerk hit a button and their items moved forward.

"That will be sixty-eight dollars and seventy-five cents," the grocery clerk said.

"That's a lot of money," Sammy exclaimed with a frown on her face.

"Yes, it is. That's why we have to watch what we put in the basket. We have to have enough money to pay for the items we want to purchase." Grammy opened her purse and took out her wallet, pulled out a plastic card, and swiped it through a machine.

"What does that machine do with your card, Grammy?"

"It allows you to buy the things we put in our basket." Grammy turned her credit card over. "See this black strip on the back of my card?"

"Yes, I see it."

"Information is coded on it, and when I swipe it through the card reader, it knows if you have enough money to pay for your items."

"Grammy, you must have lots of money."

The grocery clerked laughed at Sammy.

"No, I don't have a lot of money, Sammy, but I watch what I spend. I counted the cost of each item as we put them in the basket to be sure I would be able to pay for it."

"Oh. That's a smart thing to do."

Grammy smiled at Sammy. With bags in hand, Grammy and Sammy walked out of the store.

"Can we go to the Coach store?" Sammy asked.

"Why do you want to go there?"

"Because I like nice purses and I don't have a Coach bag."

"What do you know about a Coach bag?" Grammy asked with a puzzled look on her face. "Coach bags are very expensive."

Sammy opened her tote bag and pulled out a coin purse. She held it up for Grammy to see. "Mommy bought me a Coach coin purse for my birthday. I like purses and Mommy said that one day I will get a big Coach bag."

"It sounds as if you need to wait until your mother can buy the Coach bag for you."

Ignoring Grammy's statement, Sammy continued to beg. "Do you have enough money on your card to buy me a Coach bag?"

Grammy looked at Sammy and put her hands on her hips. "You drive a hard bargain, but you're not going to pull the wool over Grammy's eyes. Just because you want something doesn't mean you will get it."

"I understand, but today is a perfect day to get a Coach bag since we are out shopping."

Grammy looked at Sammy and smirked. She couldn't argue with that. "I'm going to take you this time, but shopping will be over once we've gone to the Coach store."

"Thanks, Grammy."

Grammy drove to the Coach store forty minutes away. Sammy's face lit up when they entered the store. Before Grammy knew it, Sammy was picking up and inspecting the purses like a little diva.

"Grammy, this one is cute," Sammy said. "It is small and has purple trim. Purple is my favorite color and it matches my coin purse. May I get it, Grammy? Please? I won't ask for anything else."

"Sammy, do you remember me telling you that these purses are expensive?"

"Yes," Sammy said, pouting just a little.

"I didn't buy an expensive purse for myself until I was a working adult. I didn't buy your mother one either until she was out of college."

Sammy poked out her lips and looked from the small Coach bag to Grammy. "I won't ask for anything else. I promise."

Grammy sighed. "I will buy it for you if it costs less than forty dollars. The tag on it says seventy dollars. Maybe you can find something smaller."

"Grammy, the tag says seventy dollars but you get fifty percent off the price." She lifted the tag so Grammy could see it better. "That means...that means," Sammy counted in her head, "it costs only thirty-five dollars. Thirty-five dollars is less than forty."

"They will add tax to the cost."

"But Grammy, this is a good deal. My mommy knows how to make a good deal, and this is one."

"Maybe you should wait until your mommy is able to buy it for you."

Water formed in the corners of Sammy's eyes. Her eyes were sad and dejected; it was an Academy-Award winning performance.

Grammy laughed in spite of herself. Once she started laughing, she couldn't stop. She wasn't sure how a ten-year old was able to squeeze her conscience like that. At first, Sammy wasn't sure why Grammy was laughing, but before long she joined in. When Grammy reached for the Coach bag and took it to the register, a great, big smile appeared on Sammy's face.

The nice cashier wrapped the Coach bag and put it in a cute white and red carry bag that had Coach written all over it. Grammy gave it to Sammy.

"Thank you, Grammy. I will take good care of my Coach bag. I can't wait to show, Mommy."

"What I'd like for you to remember about this day, Sammy, is that while shopping is fun, money doesn't grow on trees and you can't always have something because you want it."

"Yes, Grammy. You have to go to work to earn the money you spend and that some things are more important than a pretty dress and purse."

Grammy's eyes protruded from their sockets. She couldn't believe that Sammy had uttered that important thought from her mouth. "So," Grammy asked, still perplexed, "what things are more important than a pretty dress and a purse?"

Sammy giggled. "We talked about household responsibilities in my class at school."

"What grade are you in?"

"Fourth grade. The teacher said that before our parents can go out and buy iPods and Wii games, they have to pay the rent, buy groceries, and pay all the important bills like heat, water, and car notes."

"My, my, my," Grammy said, still reeling from being out-foxed by a fourth grader. "They are still teaching good family values in our schools. That's great." She patted

Sammy on the head. "You are right, and the next time you want to buy a Coach bag, you'll have to earn it."

"Yes, Grammy, I understand. You're the coolest grandma in the whole wide world. I love you."

"I love you, too, Sammy."

Grammy and Sammy returned from shopping all pooped out. Sammy took off her coat and shoes and asked Grammy for something to eat. It had been a long day, but Sammy enjoyed shopping with Grammy. Sammy looked up at Grammy and smiled.

"Now I know what you mean, Grammy, when you say shop 'til you drop."

Grammy laughed and laughed and soon Sammy joined in. "For that my dear granddaughter, I'm going to make you a big hamburger and lots of fries, just the way you like it."

"Thanks, Grammy. I love it when I come to visit you. Maybe next week we can visit the zoo."

Grammy smiled at Sammy. She was worn out, but she loved her granddaughter dearly. "If your mother says you can go to the zoo, we'll go. You should invite Rusty to come along."

"I will, Grammy. I'm so glad we moved to North Carolina."

"I look forward to our next adventure."

LESSON

Always tell the truth.

Money doesn't grow on trees. You have to earn it.

You can't have everything you want.

WHAT LESSON DID YOU LEARN?

Grammy and Sammy Go to the Zoo

Sammy woke up early in the morning. She was excited. Today she, her brother, Rusty, and Grammy were going to the zoo. It was going to take two hours to get there and Grammy said they would leave at ten o'clock or as soon as Russell, Sr. dropped off Rusty.

After Rusty arrived, Sammy and Rusty got in the back seat of Grammy's car and buckled their seatbelts. Soon, they were on their way. The North Carolina Zoo was in the city of Asheboro.

"Grammy, how much longer is it to the zoo? I'm anxious to see the animals."

"It won't be much longer, Sammy. If I were to guess, I'd say it will take us another twenty minutes."

"Twenty minutes?" Sammy said with a look of disgust on her face. "We've already been riding forever."

"You have to be patient. I have to drive the speed limit so I won't get a speeding ticket or have an accident. We want to get to the zoo in one piece."

"Yeah, Sammy," Rusty said, putting in his two cents. "We want to get there in one piece."

"I'll try to be more patient, but I'm tired of riding."

"Are you too tired to go the zoo? It requires a lot of walking and it costs money to go in. I'm not going to waste my money if you're too tired to walk around and see the exhibits."

"I'm not too tired, Grammy," Rusty said. "We can leave Sammy in the car."

"We can't leave Sammy in the car, Rusty. She's going with us no matter how tired she is. This was her idea."

"Grammy, I'm not too tired to go to the zoo. I'm excited; that's all."

Grammy smiled. "Sit back. We'll be there in no time."

When they finally arrived at the zoo, Rusty was the first to jump out of the car. They parked in the Africa section at the lower part of the zoo. Sammy wanted to see the jungle animals.

"Come on Grammy and Sammy. I can't wait."

"Hold your horses, Rusty. "You can't get inside without me."

Sammy laughed. It felt good to see Grammy scolding Rusty for a change.

They walked across the long bridge to the ticket gate, got their tickets and began their trek in the zoo. There were so many things to see that they weren't sure what to see first.

"Let's go see the lions," Sammy said, pointing the way.

Grammy and Rusty followed. It was very hot and the sun was beating down on them.

"We're here," Sammy said, as she wiped her brow. "These lions are boring. They're just lying around and being lazy."

"It's hot," Grammy said. "The heat has made them lazy. They want shade like us."

"I want to hear them roar," Rusty said, putting his three cents in. "Let's go; they're no fun."

"Let's go see the elephants," Sammy said. "Hopefully, they're not resting too."

Along the way, they saw antelopes and the lemurs that looked like the characters in the movie *Madagascar*. Zebras, deer, and antelopes were in another field that looked like an African jungle.

"Look at that long-neck giraffe," Rusty said, pointing to one that was trying to eat leaves off of a tree that was much taller than it. "His tongue keeps hitting the tip of the leaf but he can't pull it off."

"There are other trees for him to eat from," Grammy said. "Why is he trying so hard to eat leaves from that tree?"

"Maybe he's stupid...oh, here comes one now," Sammy said, moving away from the fence. "Those people are feeding it. Eww, it's licking their hands with its tongue!"

"How else do you expect for the giraffe to eat?" Grammy asked. "That's how you put food in your mouth."

"Yes, Grammy, but I'm not going to let someone else's tongue lick my hand, especially an animal."

Grammy and Rusty laughed.

"It's not funny." Sammy began to slow up. "My feet are hurting."

"Remember, you wanted to come to the zoo," Grammy said. "You're only twelve years old and should be full of energy. If anyone is tired, it should be me. I have a bad knee put I'm not quitting. We're near the elephants. We can stop and rest a moment while we look at them."

No one said a word. Everyone kept walking until they reached the elephants. There were two large, gray elephants grazing near a pool. They had small tusks and large ears.

"They're eating dirt," Sammy said, watching the elephants intently as they used their trunks to uproot grass from the ground.

"At least they aren't sleeping like half of the other animals we've seen," Rusty interjected. "Ohh, they're moving to the pool."

"Look, they are drinking water and splashing it on themselves," Sammy said.

"They're getting into the lake," Rusty said all excited.

"Eww," Sammy said, yelling out loud. "They are pooping in the lake. Those are big poop droppings."

"And now that one," Rusty pointed, "is lying in the nasty water with poop swimming all around."

"He's giving himself a shower bath with the nasty water," Grammy added. Grammy, Rusty, and Sammy laughed and laughed. "It's time to move on, children."

The trio saw a lot of wildlife, different species of flowers, and now they were coming upon the baboons. The sign read: This group of baboons are Hamadryads baboons and come from Ethiopia and surrounding areas.

There were a lot of them. They looked like one, big, gigantic family—grandfather, grandmother, father, mother, sisters, brothers, uncles, aunts, cousins, and other distant

47

relatives. There was a large baboon who was definitely the ruler of the kingdom. He manned his territory while keeping a watchful eye on the humans.

Sammy began to point excitedly. "Ohh, there's a baby baboon. He's so cute. He's jumping all over the place like a kangaroo."

"He reminds me of a spider," Rusty said. "He's so skinny and spidery."

"He's tiny," Grammy chimed in. "But mama monkey is right there to take care of him."

Sammy was fascinated. "They are entertaining. Grammy, look at those baboons over there. They look like they're at the beauty shop. They're inspecting each other's hair and picking at each other like they're getting ready to get a perm."

Grammy couldn't stop laughing. "You and your vivid imagination, but I agree with you, Sammy. That's exactly what it looks like. What they're doing is getting insects that may have crawled in their fur."

"It's making me itch," Sammy said.

"Well, it's time to go. There's a lot more to see, although we won't be able to see it all today. My knee is hurting."

"I'm hungry," Rusty said.

"Me, too, Grammy," Sammy chimed in. "I've seen enough animals today. I hope your leg is going to be all right."

"It will. Let's get something to eat and head home. It is especially hot and the two of you have been pretty good sports. Okay, lead the way."

Grammy followed her grandchildren to the snack area. She was glad that they were tired. She couldn't tell them, but she was ready to go, too.

LESSON

You have to be patient.

Be careful what you ask for.

You must follow the laws of the land.

WHAT LESSON DID YOU LEARN?

Grammy and Sammy Go to the Movies

Grammy pulled the covers over Sammy after she said her prayers and got into bed. Sammy, Grammy, and Rusty had a great day at the zoo. Russell Sr. picked up Rusty and took him home, while Sammy spent the night. Sammy was enjoying her summer break with Grammy, but in another month, school would be starting and her visits to Grammy would be weekends only.

Sammy laid her head down and immediately went to sleep. Memories of the day floated in her head—the two-horned rhino, the elephants bathing in the lake, and the large family of baboons jumping all over the place. It made her shutter, though, when she recalled the elephants rolling around in the nasty water.

Sammy began to snore lightly and all of a sudden a new picture...a new dream sprouted in her head. It was in living color. She saw all of the Muppets—Kermit the Frog, Miss Piggy, Gonzo and others. She was taking a trip with them and having so much fun.

The next morning when Sammy woke up, she jumped out of bed and found Grammy making waffles for breakfast.

"Good morning, Sammy," Grammy said.

51

"Good morning, Grammy. Guess what?"

"What has you all out of breath?" Grammy wanted to know.

"Last night, I dreamed I was with Kermit the Frog, Miss Piggy, Gonzo, and Fozzie Bear. We went on a long trip and saw a lot of interesting things."

"Chile, what did you see?"

"Grammy, we saw the Grand Canyon, Hoover Dam, the Golden Gate Bridge, Mount Rushmore and a whole lot of other places."

"You mean to tell me you traveled all the way to Arizona, Nevada, California, and South Dakota in your dreams, all in one night?"

"Yes, Grammy, it was wonderful. We flew there on a special airplane."

"I say you did. That's the only way you would be able to wake up in North Carolina this morning."

Sammy laughed and Grammy joined her.

"Grammy, *The Muppets* is playing at the movie theatre. Can we go and see it today?"

"You want to go and see the Muppets at the movie theatre when you were with them all night on your long trip? You just went to the zoo. Why don't we take a break today?"

"You don't understand, Grammy. Being with Kermit the Frog and Miss Piggy was a dream."

"I should say it was, little girl. Now, go and get washed up for breakfast."

"But Grammy, I want to experience them all over again."

"Sammy, you amaze me. You do understand that you won't be able to join in the fun other than watching them on the screen. That might be a little boring after what you told me you experienced last night."

"I won't be bored, Grammy. Even though I won't be flying all over the place with them like I was in my dream, it will be the same. I'll use my imagination and it will be as if I was with them."

"Sammy, you drive a hard bargain when you put your mind to it. You have more energy than a barrel of monkeys. I can't go like you youngsters." Grammy looked out of the window. "It's raining pretty hard outside. Maybe we should wait until another time."

"It's playing only at one o'clock today, and I sure would like to see it."

"My, my, my. You remind me so much of your mother. When she got it in her mind to do something, she wouldn't stop until she did it. Let's do this. We'll see how the weather cooperates after we eat breakfast."

"You're the greatest, Grammy. I'm going to pray real hard that the sun comes out."

Grammy smiled at her granddaughter. She loved her dearly and equally enjoyed doing things with her. It didn't take much to get Grammy to go to the movies or do the things Sammy liked within reason.

At twelve noon, the sun came out. "I guess God heard your prayers," Grammy said to Sammy. "Get your jacket and I'll take you to see *The Muppets*." They got in Grammy's car and drove to the movie theater.

Grammy bought two tickets for the movie—one for Sammy and one for herself. Sammy appreciated Grammy for taking her to the movies and bought the popcorn and drinks. The popcorn and drinks were a dollar on Tuesdays.

Sammy enjoyed the movie. She laughed and laughed. It was just like her dream but better.

When the movie was over, Sammy held Grammy's hand and went to the car. It was great hanging out at the movies with Grammy.

LESSON

Have patience.

WHAT LESSON DID YOU LEARN?

Grammy Goes to the Hospital

Grammy Sue needed surgery. She needed a knee replacement. The cartilage in her knee was worn out. The two bones that meet at the knee joint were rubbing together and made it hard for Grammy to walk.

Sammy's mother, Bridget, was upset with Grammy for not telling her that she needed surgery. Bridget is Grammy's only daughter. Grammy's son and Bridget's brother, Malcom, lived in Seattle, which is on the other side of the United States. Bridget was glad that she lived close so that she could be there for Grammy.

At five o'clock in the morning, Bridget accompanied Grammy to the hospital for her surgery. It was late July, and it was very hot outside. Bridget and Grammy watched the sun come up as they rode along.

Grammy was in surgery for four hours and in recovery for another two hours. Grammy's blood pressure was high and the doctors were trying to control it. Bridget prayed that her mother would be fine. Six hours later, the hospital staff rolled Grammy to her room on a hospital gurney. Bridget followed behind them. Grammy was still groggy and not fully awake.

When they arrived at Grammy's room and pushed the door open, Bridget was surprised to see Russell Sr., Rusty and Sammy waiting inside. Rusty and Sammy stared at Grammy and seemed a little frightened because she was not awake or moving.

The nursing staff moved Grammy to her bed. A needle was stuck in her hand with a long tube running from it that was attached to a pole with a bag of liquid hanging from it. This was called an "IV" and held some of Grammy's medicine. Another gadget was clipped to her middle finger to monitor Grammy's heart rate. The nurses promised they would be back to check on her.

"Is Grammy all right?" Sammy asked, standing a short distance away.

"Yes, she's going to be fine," Bridget said. "The doctors gave Grammy some powerful medicine to make her sleep and not feel the pain when they operated on her knee."

"Why is her leg all wrapped up if they operated only on her knee?" Rusty asked.

"The doctors opened up Grammy's knee and replaced the old one with a new one. Part of her leg had to be cut so they could do that."

"Yikes," Sammy said, wrinkling up her face. "Grammy must hurt a lot."

"That's why they gave her medicine...so she wouldn't feel it."

"How are you doing, honey?" Russell, Sr. asked Bridget.

"I'm fine. I've been praying for my mom."

"As you said, she's going to be all right."

"Mommy, when is Grammy going to wake up?" Sammy asked.

"It'll take some time for the medicine to wear off, but it won't be long."

An hour passed before Grammy began to move. She batted her eyelids and closed them again.

"Grammy, we're here," Sammy blurted out. Sammy finally moved to Grammy's side and rubbed her arm.

Grammy's eyelids fluttered and this time she opened her eyes. As her eyes adjusted to the room, she moved her head. A smile crossed her face. "Hi, everybody," she whispered. "How long have I been asleep?"

"A long time," Rusty interjected. "I was about to go to sleep." Russell, Sr. and Bridget laughed.

"I'm sorry, Rusty. The medicine they gave me made me sleepy."

"That's okay. We're glad you're all right. It's Sammy's fault for making you take us to the zoo."

"It's not my fault," Sammy retorted. "I didn't know Grammy had a bum knee."

Grammy managed a laugh. "It's no one's fault. My knee has been bad a good while, but I kept putting off the surgery. After walking around the zoo, it became obvious to me that I couldn't put it off any longer. Sammy, I'm going to need your help when I get out of the hospital."

"Huh?" Sammy said.

"We're going to have lots of fun. You'll have to get things I need; I won't be able to do a lot of walking right away. You may have to make breakfast for me and comb my hair."

Sammy looked at Bridget. "Are you coming with me, Mommy?"

"Come with you? Aren't you the one who always runs to Grammy's house because you have so much fun with her and she does all those wonderful things with you? I don't recall you asking me to tag along."

"I'm asking you now."

The whole room erupted in laughter. "I plan to stay with Grammy for a few weeks while she recovers and has to go to physical therapy."

"Oh," Sammy said, feeling better about the situation.

"You may have to change my bandage and rewrap my leg," Grammy said to Sammy.

"No, I'm not going to do that."

"What if I had said, no, I'm not going to buy you that Coach bag you have draped on your shoulder? What if I said no, Sammy, we aren't going to see *The Muppets*? What if I said, I can't take you to the zoo or the beauty shop?"

Sammy gave Grammy a puzzled look. She was quiet, possibly thinking about what her grandmother said. "But it isn't the same, Grammy. I'm too young to take care of you. I wouldn't know what to do. I might faint if I look at your leg."

Grammy stared at Sammy and started laughing. "You're a piece of work, Sammy. You are my daughter's child."

"Okay, Mom," Bridget said. "There is no way that I was as feisty as Sammy when I was growing up."

"Oh, you were."

Rusty and Russell, Sr. laughed.

"I'm sleepy. Do I have your word that you'll be there to help me when I get out of the hospital, Sammy?"

"Yes, Grammy, Mommy and I will be there to help you."

When Sammy looked up at Grammy, she was fast asleep. Sammy wasn't sure Grammy heard her answer. Whether she heard or not, Sammy was going to help Grammy with her recovery.

LESSON

Do for others; it's not always about you.

WHAT DID LESSON DID YOU LEARN?

Sammy Owes the Library:
The Case of the Missing Library Book

After Grammy was released from the hospital, Sammy and her mother, Bridget, went to stay with Grammy for a month while she recovered from her surgery. Sammy helped Grammy, too. Eventually, Bridget had to go home and see about Russell, Sr. and Rusty.

Today, Grammy had to go to physical therapy, and she was all pooped out when she finished. Sammy fell asleep but Grammy was still awake but not moving very fast.

The telephone rang. It was Sammy's mother, Bridget. The telephone woke Sammy up.

"Sammy, can you come here please?" Grammy called out. Sammy slowly trudged to Grammy's room.

"Yes," Sammy said, half awake, as she entered Grammy's room.

"Your mother called and said that she received a phone call from the library about an overdue book. She wants you to come home and find the book."

Sammy was scared. She knew what book her mother was talking about. She'd been looking for the book for two weeks. The book was a Junie B. Jones book, *Jingle Bells, Batman Smells (P.S. so Does May)*.

Slowly, Sammy walked to where Grammy sat, holding the phone out to her. Scared out of her wits, Sammy took the phone from Grammy and put it to her ear.

"Mommy," Sammy said, her voice shaking like a leaf, "Grammy said you want to talk to me."

"Yes. I received a phone call from the library today, and they said you have an overdue book that is going to cost a late fee of five dollars. It's one of your Junie B. books. Why didn't you take it to the library when we were there several days ago?"

"I was still reading it and I wanted to finish it."

"You could have renewed it. Where is the book now?"

"In my room," Sammy whispered.

The truth was that the book was lost; she couldn't find it.

"I'm coming to pick you up now so that you can find the book. You won't be going to Grammy's house for a while."

"Mommy, Grammy needs me. I'll come home right now and look for the book. I'll do extra chores to make up for the cost of the overdue book."

"Have your things ready. I'm coming to get you now."

"Can I come back to Grammy's house?"

"No, you won't be able to go to Grammy's tonight. You're going to stay home and do some chores to pay for your overdue book. I hope you find it."

Sammy hung up the phone and looked at Grammy. "I'm sorry, Grammy. I'll come back as soon as I can."

"Don't worry about me, baby. Grammy will be all right. You better find that book or your mother won't let you come back."

In the next hour, Bridget was at Grammy's front door. Bridget hugged and kissed her mother and made sure she was all right before she and Sammy left to go home.

There was silence all the way home. The only thing Sammy could hear was her mother breathing hard and she didn't want to talk about the book. Sammy lied about knowing where the book was and prayed that it was somewhere in the house.

As soon as they arrived home, Sammy dashed to her room. She looked high and low and on her shelves but couldn't find the book. Next, she dropped to her knees and looked under the bed, but it wasn't there either. Sammy looked under her covers, behind the bed, in all of her drawers but failed to find the book.

Sammy sat on the edge of her bed and began to cry. She wouldn't be able to go back to Grammy's if she didn't find the book.

Wiping her eyes dry, Sammy got up and went to the kitchen. She passed Rusty's room.

"What's wrong with you, Sammy?" Rusty called out to her.

"None of your business."

Rusty went to the door. "You don't have to be mean. I was only asking."

"I can't find my library book," Sammy said. She turned around and went into Rusty's room. "Mommy is going to ground me and I won't be able to go to Grammy's house anymore."

"That's not going to happen. Mommy can't keep you away from Grammy."

"What do you know?"

"Trust me; I know. Now, what's the name of the book you're looking for?"

Sammy sat down on the end of Rusty's bed. It's the Junie B. Jones book, *Jingle Bells, Batman Smells!*"

"Why didn't you say so?"

"What do you mean by that, Rusty?" Sammy asked accusingly.

"I have your book. I read it and forgot to put it back in your room."

Sammy screamed at Rusty. "I'm in a lot of trouble because of that book. Give it to me right now. I'm going to tell Mommy you had it all this time."

"I may have had it all this time, but it was your responsibility."

"Shut up, Rusty, and give me the book. I've got to take it to the library right away. Every day it's late costs Mommy more money."

Rusty crossed the room to his dirty clothes basket and retrieved the book from underneath a pile of dirty clothes. "Here it is."

Sammy was happy to get the book, but she was angry at Rusty for taking it without her permission. She took the book and went to find her mother.

When Bridget saw Sammy with the book, her eyes brightened. "Where was the book?"

"It was in Rusty's dirty clothes basket."

"Rusty's dirty clothes basket? How did it get there?"

"He took it without my permission and forgot to put it back."

"Hmm," Bridget said. "Do you remember the cell phone incident? This is what happens when we take things that don't belong to us without asking. That's a lesson to you in reverse, although I will have a long talk with Rusty. If we hurry, we can get to the library and turn the book in before it closes.

"Sammy, let this be a lesson to you. Although it wasn't your fault that you couldn't find the book, it was your responsibility to keep up with it. Rusty will have to pay the fine."

"Yes!" Sammy said, jumping for joy. "Does this mean I can go back to Grammy's tonight?"

"Not so fast, young lady. You're going to spend tonight at home. School will be starting soon and tomorrow we're going shopping for school clothes."

Sammy sighed. "Okay, Mommy. After we're done shopping, can I go to Grammy's house?"

"Yes, you can go to Grammy's. I'm glad that you and Grammy get along so well. Now get a sweater; it's cool outside."

Bridget and Sammy went to the library and turned in the missing book. Sammy's mother paid the fine.

"Can I check out a book?" Sammy asked. "I have my library card with me."

"One book." Bridget hugged Sammy and gave her a big kiss on the top of her head. And then Sammy was off to find a book.

LESSON

Always tell the truth.

You must be responsible.

Always ask before taking something that doesn't belong to you.

WHAT LESSON DID YOU LEARN?

Grammy and Sammy's Tea Party

Today, Sammy was bored. She had nothing to do and everyone else seemed to be occupied with their own thing. Sammy asked her brother, Rusty, to play cards, but he had homework and didn't have time to play.

Sammy had an idea. She would call Grammy to see if they could do something fun together. Sammy asked her mother if she could call Grammy.

"Yes, Sammy, you may call Grammy."

Sammy was excited. Her eyes lit up when her mother gave her the cell phone.

"Hi, Grammy, this is Sammy."

"This is a pleasant surprise," Grammy said. "Why would my favorite granddaughter be calling me today?"

"Grammy," Sammy said softly, "I'm bored. I want to do something fun and no one has time for me today."

"So I guess you want to come to Grammy's house to see what you can do exciting over here. Am I right?"

"How did you guess?" Sammy snickered.

"I know my granddaughter well."

Sammy laughed out loud, and before long Grammy laughed too. "You are right, Grammy. May I come over?"

"Yes, you may, Sammy. I've just thought of something."

"What is it, Grammy?" Sammy asked with excitement in her voice.

"Why don't we have a tea party?"

"Oh, that would be so much fun."

"Go ask your mother if it's all right for you to come over."

"I know she will say yes."

"You must ask her first."

"Okay, Grammy. I will."

"If your mother says you can come, Grammy will take you shopping and buy you the prettiest dress with shoes to match, gloves and a cute little hat to sit on your head. Would you like that?"

"Can I come now, Grammy?"

"What are you going to do first, Sammy?

"Ask Mommy if I can come to your house."

"All right, I hope to see you soon."

Four hours later, Sammy's mother, Bridget, drove her to Grammy's house and dropped her off. Grammy was waiting at the door with her purse on her arm. Grammy waved to Bridget.

Grammy drove to a specialty dress shop for young girls. Sammy was in awe at all the pretty dresses in the store. She selected a lavender taffeta dress. It had an empire waist with white flowers bordering it and the collar. Grammy bought her a pair of white gloves and a white straw hat. Now they were ready for their tea party.

When they arrived at Grammy's house, Grammy changed her clothes and put on a pretty peach-colored spring dress. She set the table for two and on small platters, she placed chicken salad sandwiches with the crust cut off, pink iced cookies cut in the shape of a heart, and chocolate dipped strawberries.

"Yum," Sammy said as she watched Grammy put the food on the table. "When did you have time to make all of this?"

"After I found out what time your mother was bringing you over, I boiled the chicken and when it was done, I prepared the chicken salad. I didn't have quite enough time to make the cookies or the chocolate covered strawberries, so I ran to my favorite bakery and purchased them."

"This is so cool."

Then Grammy brought out a glass pitcher filled with raspberry ginger ale and a teapot full of sweetened herbal tea.

"Wow," Sammy said. "This is the best tea party I've ever been to."

"It's probably the only tea party you've been to," Grammy said with a chuckle. Sammy laughed.

Sammy picked up her tea cup with her pinky finger sticking out. Then she placed sandwiches on her plate and waited for Grammy to do the same.

"This is so much fun," Sammy said, as her white straw hit tipped below her eyes.

"You look like a princess, Sammy. You are so beautifful. Let me get my camera so I can take a picture."

"Thank you for the tea party, Grammy."

LESSON

Always ask permission to do something that requires your parent(s) say so.

WHAT LESSON DID YOU LEARN?

Samayya Walters "Sammy"   Suzetta Perkins "Grammy"